JOHANNES BRAHMS

QUINTET

for Clarinet, 2 Violins, Viola and Violoncello
B minor/h-Moll/Si mineur
Op. 115

Edited by/Herausgegeben von
Philip Cranmer

Ernst Eulenburg Ltd

London · Mainz · Madrid · New York · Paris · Prague · Tokyo · Toronto · Zürich

Revised edition

© 1982 Ernst Eulenburg Ltd, London

Ernst Eulenburg Ltd, 48 Great Marlborough Street,
London W1V 2BN

JOHANNES BRAHMS

Quintet for clarinet and strings in B minor, Op. 115

Brahms's erstwhile pupil and discerning friend, Elisabeth von Herzogenberg, had enthused to him about the artistry of Richard Mühlfeld, first clarinettist in the Meiningen Court Orchestra, since the early 1880s. But it was not until Brahms accepted a joint invitation from the Duke himself and Hans von Bülow, the orchestra's conductor, to regard Meiningen as a second home and trying-out ground for new works, that through Mühlfeld's playing he came to realise the clarinet's full potential and how much its hauntingly romantic, dark-hued timbre accorded with his own mood of autumnal nostalgia as gradually he approached the age of sixty and one by one his closest friends were dying. Even as he wrote the Quintet, Elisabeth von Herzogenberg herself was overtaken by the heart disease so soon to kill her. The work was completed in 1891 at Ischl, by now Brahms's favourite mountain retreat, shortly after the Trio for clarinet, cello and piano, Op. 114. Brahms's final tribute to Mühlfeld, the two Clarinet Sonatas of Op. 120, did not emerge until 1894. The Quintet was first tried out at a private party in Meiningen on 24 November, 1891, with Brahms's old friend, Joachim, playing first violin alongside Mühlfeld. The official première from Mühlfeld and the Joachim Quartet followed in Berlin on 12 December, 1891.

Rarely in his output did Brahms achieve a mellower fusion of heart and head. While flooded with compassionate awareness of life's transience, the music at the same time is a miracle of disciplined economy, with more subtle thematic inter-relationships and metamorphoses than in any other chamber work from his pen.

The Quintet has a prevailing mood of bitter-sweetness, epitomised by the first movement's opening subject, a sigh for all things loved and lost; while in the middle of the slow movement Brahms seems to recall the music-making of Hungarian gypsies, so dear to him in his youth.

The third movement brings yet another reminder of Brahms's attitude to the Scherzo as he grew older, with the high-powered Beethovenian drive of former days ceding to something at once more lyrical, gracious and intimate. Here he begins with a flowing Andantino (briefly recalled at the end) before embarking on the Scherzo proper.

For the finale Brahms reverts to variation form, regarded by many of his contemporaries as his hall-mark. In a final masterstroke he recalls the work's opening theme in quietly resigned, sombre farewell.

Joan Chissell

JOHANNES BRAHMS

Quintett für Klarinette und Streicher, h-Moll, Op. 115

Die einstige Schülerin und verständnisvolle Freudin von Brahms, Elisabeth von Herzogenberg, hatte ihm begeistert von den künstlerischen Fähigkeiten Richard Mühlfelds erzählt, der im letzten Jahrhundert seit Anfang der achtziger Jahre Soloklarinettist bei der Meininger Hofkapelle war. Doch erst als Brahms vom Fürsten selbst im Einvernehmen mit dem Dirigenten des Orchesters, Hans von Bülow, eingeladen wurde, Meiningen als seine zweite Heimat anzusehen und dort seine neuen Werke auszuprobieren, wurde er sich durch Mühlfelds Spiel ganz der Ausdrucksmöglichkeiten der Klarinette bewusst, deren unvergesslicher, romantischer und dunkler Klang seiner eigenen herbstlichen Stimmung entsprach, denn er war damals bald sechzig Jahre alt, und seine nächsten Freunde starben einer nach dem anderen. Ja, als er schon mit der Arbeit am Quintett begonnen hatte, wurde Elisabeth von Herzogenberg von einem Herzleiden befallen, das sie in Kürze hinraffen sollte. Das Werk wurde 1891 in Ischl, seinem inzwischen bevorzugten Zufluchtsort in den Bergen, vollendet, und zwar kurz nach dem Trio für Klarinette, Cello und Klavier, Op. 114. Der letzte Tribut, den Brahms der Kunst Mühlfelds zollte, weren die beiden Klarinettensonaten Op. 120, die ihre Gestaltung erst 1894 erhielten. Das Quintett wurde zuerst am 24. November 1891 privat in Meiningen ausprobiert, wobei Joachim, der ein alter Freund von Brahms war, neben Mühfeld die erste Geige spielte. Die offizielle Premiere mit Mühlfeld und dem Joachim-Quartett folgte in Berlin am 12. Dezember 1891.

Selten hat Brahms in seinen Werken eine weichere Verschmelzung von Herz und Geist erreicht. Während die Musik von einem mitfühlenden Wissen über die Vergänglichkeit des Lebens durchflutet ist, stellt sie gleichzeitig ein Wunder von disziplinierter Sparsamkeit dar und hat feinsinnigere Verwandlungen und Beziehungen zwischen den Themen als irgendein anderes seiner Kammermusikwerke.

Im Quintett herrscht sine bittersüsse Stimmung vor, für die schon das Thema zu Anfang des ersten Satzes typisch ist – ein Seufzer ist es, der alle geliebten und verlorenen Dinge beklagt, während Brahms in der Mitte des langsamen Satzes an das Musizieren ungarischer Zigeuner zu erinnern scheint, das ihm in seiner Jugend so sehr am Herzen lag.

Im dritten Satz werden wir noch einmal daran erinnert, wie sich Brahms das Scherzo vorstellte, als er älter wurde, denn hier weicht das gewaltige Voranstürmen im Sinne Beethovens, das einer früheren Zeit angehört, etwas Neuem, das lyrischer, und zugleich anmutiger und intimer ist. In diesem Satz fängt Brahms mit einem fliessenden Andantino an (woran er kurz am Ende erinnert), bevor er das eigentliche Scherzo beginnt.

Im Finale geht Brahms auf die Variationsform zurück, die bei vielen seiner Zeitgenossen als die typischste Ausdrucksform seines Genies galt. Ein letzter meisterlicher Zug ist die Erinnerung an das Anfangsthema des Werks, das nun in stiller Entsagung wie ein trauriger Abschied klingt.

Joan Chissell
Übersetzung Stefan de Haan

QUINTET

I

Johannes Brahms, Op. 115
1833-1897

No.239

EE 6725

Edited by Philip Cranmer
© 1982 Ernst Eulenburg Ltd, London

4

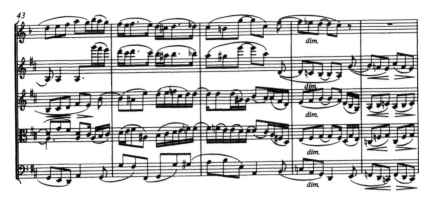

EE 6725

Quasi sostenuto

12

EE 6725

EE 6725

14

II

24

EE 6725

25

III

Presto non assai, ma con sentimento

EE 6725

IV

Con moto

42

44

179

189

197 **Un poco meno mosso**